Coaching Reflections

Venture *publications*

John Banks

Front cover: Quintessentially mid-sixties British, but the foreign manufacturers were gearing up for a determined sales push in the UK. Black & White Motorways 1967 Leyland Leopard **L287** (**KDD 287E**) was in Nottingham in May 1971. Its 47-seat coachwork was by Plaxton. (*G H F Atkins/© John Banks Collection*)

Rear cover: By 1975 that initiative was really beginning to produce results. Volvo and Mercedes chassis were in British fleets, and in that year **JNK 554N**, a DAF with Duple 55-seat coachwork, thought to be the first British-registered DAF, entered service with Robinson of Appleby. (*John Banks Collection*)

Title page: A typical late 1970s collection of lightweight coaches includes **RSY 972M**, a 45-seat Bedford YRQ new in August 1973 to Killar, of Dalkeith; **JUA 326E**, a 1967 Bedford VAM5 45-seater ex-Wallace Arnold; **LJH 248L**, a Bedford YRT with 53 seats, which had been new to Limebourne Coaches in 1973; and **EXD 520J**, another 53-seater, a 1971 Ford R226 from the batch EXD 511-22J new to Hillside, of Luton, in March 1971. RSY 972M was bodied by Duple, the rest by Plaxton. (*Geoff Coxon*)

Below: Industrial cranes alongside the River Hull in the city of Kingston upon Hull tower over a selection of B10M Volvos, all bodied by Van Hool, in the fleet of Halcyon Travel. For the four vehicles, four completely different livery schemes were used - and there were other variations. This is a 1987 view and the vehicles had all come off the North Sea Ferries overnight crossing morning arrivals from either Zeebrugge or Rotterdam and after cleaning and refuelling would go out again that same night on tours to Brussels, Paris, Amsterdam and Cologne. (*John Banks*)

>> *Opposite page:* Long-distance night travel by coach always had a certain aura for the passenger and conditions for the drivers were easier than during the day. A United Automobile Services Leyland Leopard waits to leave on the long haul from Newcastle to London in 1978. (*Geoff Coxon*)

INTRODUCTION

In the late 1960s the writer began to feel the urge to leave a settled and secure career in the police service, with its prospect of early retirement in his mid-forties on a good pension, to work in the uncertain world of the passenger transport industry. Trouble was, it became evident that the word "uncertain" in this context was a little like referring to a nuclear explosion as "a disturbance". The move - eventually made in 1972 - was irrevocable and a mistake (in the sense that a hobby does not always translate into a profession with much success) but the best had to be, and was, made of it. The reader need not fear, however, that a boring autobiography is to be presented in these pages. Rather, a series of reflections, and a selection of photographs, will attempt to paint a picture of what coaching did and does, of how it was and is done, and of the machinery used to do it. Suffice it to restrict the autobiographical elements to anecdotal comment and - important, this - to stress that the writer worked both in the cab and in traffic management; he hopes therefrom to present a balanced picture, warts and all. As was the case with Cromwell's portrait, the warts will not be painted over.

The coaching industry was, and no doubt still is, a very different animal from that which the enthusiast pictures from his fleet lists, number-recording and picture-taking activities. Even *entrée* to the hallowed and otherwise inaccessible offices of an operator for authorised research for an article or book being prepared does not give the full story, and talking to inspectors, or drivers and conductors - "platform staff" or "road personnel", to quote just two of management's various appellations for the people who actually earned the profits - certainly does not.

The human interest of operating on hire on a stage-carriage service along a set of country lanes where passengers (usually only one) alighted at each farm, cottage or lane-end; the ease with which cities hundreds of miles apart could be visited along motorways at - when it was legal - 70 or more miles per hour (90 or even 100, indeed, in the case of Midland Red); the delight of seeing new places on a tour of Scotland or Wales or the Lake District; the mystery and strangeness of driving along the "wrong" side of the road on continental European roads; the humour, not to mention the anxiety, of negotiating customs posts (in western Europe now largely a thing of the past) and struggling with the language and officialdom; battling with apparently insane drivers in Paris or Rome and quickly realising that "when in Rome do as the Romans do" was the only way to survive: none of these, told as anecdotes by the people who were involved, reach the often dramatic, seldom smooth, story of what went on behind the scenes.

"Behind the scenes" was often nothing more than the other side of the wall separating the garage from the traffic manager's or general manager's office. That the translation of careers was not going to be an easy one came on the first morning as Traffic Manager when it became clear that for a fleet of 36 public service vehicles there were but eleven drivers on the payroll. Question to General Manager: "Where do the rest of the drivers come from?" Answer: "Don't know old chap. I've been here only a fortnight myself. I think we use part-timers." It slowly began to dawn that one of the first - nay! the very first - questions that should have been asked during the job interview, or at the very latest before accepting the post, was "why did the previous incumbent leave?" And, had one known, the second should have been "and why did *your* predecessor leave?" Perhaps another, at an interview on a Wednesday, should have been an enquiry as to why no candidate not able to start the following Monday would be considered. I could, and did. We live and learn.

Thirty-six public service vehicles employed from 5.00am to gone midnight on morning and evening works contracts, morning and afternoon school contracts, private hires during the day and in the evenings, extended tours, continental holidays, not to mention the odd stage-carriage service or two, cannot be run with eleven drivers, nor even - legally - with 36 and, at a time when the possession of a PSV licence guaranteed work, it was not easy. From frantic telephone calls to competitors (friends and, at desperate need, sometimes enemies) to "hire in" it soon became obvious that others were in the same straits and that this was how much of the industry ran. Apart from anything else, there were the Drivers' Hours Regulations. These were known and understood - especially that there were two different sets, British and European, *both legal and in use* - from the earlier career, but said earlier experience was a powerful antidote to the attitude "drivers' hours? Ignore 'em!".

And then there were the vehicles. They came in various seating capacities - from 29 to 57 in the writer's charge at that time - and it was easy to forget that otherwise identical vehicles differed only in that, for example, one might be "a 51" and another "a 49". And did the organiser asking for a 30-seater really have 30 people, or was it just a case of her and her 22 fellow shoppers-to-London not wanting a 29-seat Bedford VAS for the trip to the Capital? One practice speedily suppressed by the new incumbent was that of quoting for sizes of coach that the fleet did not contain. Then there was the group of 51 that had booked a 50-seater: "But it's only one extra. They are all 51-seaters these days, aren't they?" No, they were not, and the extra sat on the floor.

Although coaches were by then superficially very similar in external appearance, in their mechanical and interior specifications vehicle types differed greatly. Organisers might not, in fact, have known a Bedford VAS from a Bedford CA van, or a Ford Thames from a Ford Transit, but they very quickly found out which made all that noise from the funny hump at the front, which struggled raucously along at a maximum 49 miles per hour and which cruised at 70. Drivers knew, too: failure dockets on lightweights, particularly in respect of the smaller and older ones ten minutes before they were due to go out and there was an AEC Reliance or a Volvo B58 standing spare in a corner, had to be examined closely for accuracy.

Coaches could be new or somebody else's cast-offs. Purchasing policies for new vehicles might encompass lightweights to be disposed of after a season or two and a leavening of Leopards or Volvos that would last for much longer. Smaller, less affluent operators perforce obliged to buy second-hand lightweights had the worst of all worlds and there were, frankly, vehicles on the road that should not have been.

And that was the coaching industry: from the twelve-year old SB5 or Thames Trader fuming and banging down the M1 to a football match, lending a whole new meaning to the expression "to travel hopefully is better than to arrive", to the brand-new Volvo, DAF or Leopard parked proudly underneath the Eiffel Tower; from the pristine Bristol RE or Leyland Tiger effortlessly linking Middlesbrough, Manchester or Maidstone with the Capital to the past-its-sell-by-date six-wheeled Bedford VAL hired in to duplicate on a bigger operator's over-subscribed service; from the 25 couples of the Fine Arts Society who asked for a non-smoking driver and classical music through the speakers for their trip to Paris to the unspeakably obscene drinking party from Oldham to Hamburg who left the coach looking and smelling worse than the council refuse dump - they all took their places on a large canvas, a canvas whose whole area could seldom be seen by one individual: the driver often recked little of the trauma associated with management's struggles in writing up a traffic schedule in the busy season; management, if the truth be told, sometimes knew - and cared - even less about the driver's problems; passengers seldom cared about either, sometimes wrote in with compliments if all went well, more often didn't bother, and even more often complained bitterly when the last degree of perfection was not attained under even the most impossible of circumstances.

But we loved it - well, most of the time. Let us take a look at the vehicles - from the fleets of the independents, large and small, the BET and the BTC, and even some municipalities, as well as a few

from abroad - and the services, the tours, the excursions upon which they worked.

Sources and acknowledgements

The illustrations are all from the writer's collection, and include many taken by Geoffrey Atkins and by the late Geoff Coxon - in each case a guarantee of excellence. It is Geoff Coxon's work with colour film, indeed, that has inspired this volume. Since, in partnership with another enthusiast, acquiring Geoff's collection, the writer has come to realise that Geoff - an award-winning photographer - produced work that is the equal of any and superior to most; it is not inappropriate to speak of Geoff Coxon and Geoffrey Atkins in the same breath.

To the work of the two Geoffs has been added a judiciously chosen selection from the writer's collection, some of it not originally enthusiast-orientated and offering a different slant on the world of coaching.

The writer has, as ever, sought and received unstintingly given help over vehicle details from Ron Maybray, to whom grateful thanks. Thanks also to Mary and Dave Shaw for reading the proofs, and to all the wonderful, friendly, helpful characters who made the writer's time in the industry so interesting and - at times - funny, not to say hilarious. With hindsight, I would not do it again; with foreknowledge, indeed, I would not have done it then, but it was certainly an experience. To the "characters" of the other sort, well - most of them are forgiven if not forgotten: just a few are forgotten most of the time but not, ever, forgiven.

John Banks
Romiley, Cheshire
July, 2005

This and << opposite pages: The period 1900 to 1935 saw a development from what were basically crudely motorised horse-drawn vehicles to the halfcab motor coach and the following three and a half decades a move to underfloor-engined boxes on wheels that all but eclipsed the halfcab. More recent times have been much more stable and superficially - especially to the untutored eye - there is not all that much difference between York Pullman's late-1970s Bedford VAM **RDN 405P** and Premiere Travel of Nottingham's up to the minute marvel on a Volvo chassis (**LUI 7668**). Thirty-five years apart, they were both doing the same job: transporting private hire groups, respectively to the Lake District and Lincoln. *(Geoff Coxon; John Banks [2])*

Survivors from an earlier era by the nineteen-sixties were often still there because they filled a specific need for which a more modern chassis was not available, this being particularly so of the 25- to 29-seat class, in which the demise of the Bedford OB in 1950, of which more below, coincided with the OB's competitors in this class, for example the Austin and Commer equivalents, also being phased out. Thus such vehicles were frequently operated longer than might have been the case had replacements been readily available and this happily led to a number of them surviving into preservation. **VY 9624** *(left)*, a 1937 Waveney-bodied 25-seat Bedford WTB, was new to York Pullman as fleet number 34 in 1934. Sold to Bentley of Kirbymoorside in 1948, it ran for a further 19 years. At right is another Bedford WTB, this time a Duple-bodied 26-seater dating from 1939. In the previous year Bedford had restyled the WTB, the most obvious outward evidence being in the new front, which was to become very familiar on the succeeding OB. **JR 9337** was new in 1939 to C R Robson, of Smelting Syke. *(Both: Geoff Coxon)*

The Bedford OB was only just a prewar production and did not appear in great numbers until after the end of the war, although during the conflict it formed the basis for the austerity OWB service-bus version. During the second half of the 1940s, once the British motor industry was in a position to honour orders from home customers, the OB became very popular. A classic example, with the equally popular Vista 29-seat coachwork to Duple design, is **HTC 661**, which had been new in June 1947 to Gilbert, of Morecambe. This vehicle's body number (43493) is in the Duple series, but it was built under subcontract by SMT. In this charming 1979 view at the Tanfield preserved railway the vehicle was owned by Calvary Coaches and it survives in preservation. *Another type of survivor* was the big-company heavy-duty coach finding further use with an independent, in this case an ex-Maidstone and District Harrington-bodied 32-seat AEC Regal III. **KKK 840** was new in early 1949, withdrawn in 1961, sold to Braybrooke of Swaffham and, after giving several years of further service, had been scrapped by the end of 1969. The photograph was taken in August 1968. *(Both: Geoff Coxon)*

BRAYBROOKE'S

KKK 840

11

Conversion as a towing wagon or for other non-PSV use was a further way in which early coaches could survive beyond their passenger-carrying days, albeit in this case for only about a year. **HDN 583** was a slightly newer AEC Regal III, dating from 1953, and it had a Barnaby 35-seat front-entrance coach body. Number **62** in the York Pullman fleet, HDN was withdrawn in August 1969. Although then used as a towing vehicle it did not last long and was scrapped in November 1970. A pity! But then, they cannot all be preserved ... It was photographed at Scarborough, looking very dated alongside a 1961 Burlingham-bodied Leyland Tiger Cub and a Duple Yeoman-bodied Ford Thames.

Preservation is the ultimate means of survival and no vehicle is more welcome in that category than **JYC 855**, a 1948 Leyland Tiger PS1/1 with Harrington 33-seat coachwork. Delivered new to Porlock Blue Motors it was by 1960 No. **68** in the fleet of Mulley of Ixworth painted, as seen in this August 1968 view, in Corona Coaches livery. It is now preserved by an owner in Little Waltham, Essex. *(Both: Geoff Coxon)*

The Leyland Comet CPO1, because most of them had a bonnet and around 28 to 33 seats, is often thought of as being a competitor for the Bedford OB. Produced from 1948 to 1952, it also appeared as a forward-control version seating up to 38 and thus was a direct competitor to the Bedford SB as well as the OB. Leyland had the Tiger, which was about to be made obsolete by the underfloor-engined designs shortly to emerge, and its attempt to promote the Comet can only be described as a failure. Not that there was anything wrong with it, and anything an OB or SB could do a Comet could do as well or better, but as Alan Townsin has so memorably put it: Leyland's "engineering quality came with a price and few were sold". **KSM 836** (*above*) was new in 1950 to Green, of Lochmaben. In this undated seaside view it had passed to an operator named Atkinson.

Front-engined coaches could be given a more modern appearance with fully fronted coachwork. This ex-Maidstone & District Beadle-Leyland of 1952, **OKP 973**, with Beadle 35-seat coachwork, passed to Pickering of Blackhall in 1960, with whom it is seen in another seaside view, this one taken in 1961. (*Both: Geoff Coxon*)

Leyland's underfloor-engined designs, once in production, sold so well that Leyland had no need to worry about competing in the circa 30-seat market. The massively engineered Royal Tiger and its more refined successor the Tiger Cub kept Leyland's coach order books full. The major coachbuilders sold their products on both sorts of chassis - forward-engined lightweights as well as the new generation of heavyweight underfloor-engined machines - and one of the most attractive profiles to grace the Leyland Tiger Cub was the Duple Donnington, in this case *(above)* a 41-seater in the Sunderland District fleet. Number **300** (**10 BPT**) was a 1958 acquisition and lasted until 1973.

The classic Duple design for the Bedford SB is considered by many to have been the Vega with what came to be referred to as the "butterfly grille", a coach that became very popular in the mid 1950s. **ODL 48** was an example that went into a major company fleet when it became Southern Vectis **235** in 1957. This one was a real survivor: bought by Henry Hulley & Sons Ltd, of Baslow, for spares in July 1971, it was placed in service as No. **9** in May 1973. *(Both: Geoff Coxon)*

Lightweight lifespan could on occasion equal or exceed that of heavier chassis, and this Bedford SB1 *(above)* was in service with three owners for around 18 years. New in July 1958 to Bream, of Hemel Hempstead, **554 DNK** was a Thurgood-bodied 39-seater that in 1968 passed to W Norfolk & Sons, of Nayland, with whom it was photographed in August of that year bound for Colchester. Norfolk withdrew the vehicle in 1976.

Bostock of Congleton had a striking livery that on at least one occasion suffered the somewhat mixed compliment of being minutely copied by another independent (said copier's response was "I didn't see your name on the paint tin"). The colours looked particularly attractive *(right)* on the Plaxton Consort IV coachwork on **765 JTU**, that had been new in 1960. This was another long-lived Bedford SB1, this photograph dating from September 1978. *(Both: Geoff Coxon)*

The replacement for the legendary Bedford OB was a while coming. The OB, usually with Duple Vista bodywork, had been for many operators the automatic - almost the only, indeed - choice for a 29-seater and it was a hard act to follow when it went out of production towards the end of 1950. The SB, initially a 33-seater but which gradually became bigger, was not universally accepted as an OB replacement and there remained a niche market for a 29-seater. By 1961 operators who had kept OBs in service were urgently needing to replace them and Bedford were just in time with the new VAS chassis in 1961. In true OB tradition, coachwork often to be seen on the VAS came from Duple and had 29 seats, typified by **1910 ET** *(left)* in the fleet of Riley of Rotherham, a petrol-engined VAS2 variant, which had entered service in 1962.

Even smaller coaches were needed on occasion and Bedford found many customers for the J2, a converted normal-control truck chassis. The modification to forward-control configuration was sometimes done by Bedford, sometimes by the coachbuilder. Battersby - Silver Grey, of Morecambe, had **NTJ 943G** with Plaxton 20-seat coachwork *(right)*. The coach was a still-smart ten-year-old when photographed in September 1978. The odd appearance of the narrow front track of the truck chassis combined with the 8ft-wide bodywork is well shown. *(Both: Geoff Coxon)*

Independent fleets, though on average containing a higher percentage of lightweights than those of the company operators, nevertheless had their share of interesting heavyweights, many of them away from the Leopard/Reliance beaten track. The 1967 picture *(above)* of vehicles in the fleet of Harper Brothers, Heath Hayes, juxtaposes

No. **57** (**1291 RE**), a 1959 Willowbrook-bodied Guy Arab LUF 41-seater, with Duple-bodied Bedford VAM14 No. **80** (**VBF 406D**) of 1966. The Guy was withdrawn in 1971. Despite its luxurious seating, it had just come in off stage-carriage duties. An example of the longevity that smaller operators could expect from the more

substantially built models is that of **YVA 872**, a 1961 AEC Reliance in the fleet of Hunter Brothers of Tantobie *(right)*. The Duple-bodied 41-seater had been new to Hutchinson, of Overtown, and was a healthy-looking 18 years of age when this bleak midwinter photograph was taken. *(Both: Geoff Coxon)*

An early attempt to compete with the underfloor-engined layout by making a lightweight chassis suitable for driver-only operation involved moving the front axle backwards and placing the entrance ahead of it in a design from the coachbuilder Yeates of Loughborough with the 44-seat Pegasus, based on a modified Bedford SB5, of which 1962's dual-purpose example **943 AWR** *(above)* was new to the Doncaster independent Store (Reliance), of Stainforth, but had been sold to Elsey, of Gosberton in Lincolnshire, by the time of this photograph. The Ford R192 of ten years later had refined the concept, as shown by 1972 Willowbrook-bodied 45-seater **AOD 595L** in the fleet of Devon operator Bruce and Roberts, of Lewdown, seen *(right)* in a Lake District traffic jam in 1979. *(Both: Geoff Coxon)*

Holiday contrasts are an aspect of the coaching scene that often present the vehicles of a familiar operator in more exotic surroundings. Of all fleets, that of Barton Transport is the one that could perhaps best be described as "exotic" without its owner going to the trouble of sending vehicles to - in this case - Scarborough, Scotland and Switzerland. A fleet known equally for its varied selection of second-hand double-deckers and for its flamboyant coaches, not the least point of interest about it was that one of the latter might be on local stage-carriage services during the week and at the weekend be heading for the seaside or on its way across the Channel. AEC Reliance No. **936** (**99 GAL**), a Harrington-bodied 41-seater dating from 1960, was in Scarborough *(above)* in July 1963 on its way to Scotland, an interesting enough destination though perhaps not as dramatically exciting as that reached two years later by Barton's ex-Robin Hood Coaches No. **933** (**239 CNN**), another 41-seat Reliance, this time a 1959 Duple example *(right)*, here ceding first place to the Swiss scenery. *(Both: G H F Atkins/© John Banks Collection)*

But what of the definition of a "coach" if these vehicles qualify? Yet qualify they do, as members of London's Green Line fleet, which handled the biggest urban limited-stop network in the United Kingdom under the auspices originally of the London General Omnibus Company and then of London Transport in its various incarnations for almost exactly four decades. Even when Green Line vehicles were little or even no different from service buses, for example the Green Line RTs used on the East London services into Aldgate, they were always referred to as "coaches". The splendid T-class front-entrance AEC Regals of 1930/1 were more comfortable than service bus members of the same class but the postwar AEC Regal IVs of the RF class betrayed less difference, albeit the seat cushions were deeper than on standard bus RFs. The types are represented by the preserved Duple-bodied **T219** (**GK 5486**) in a May 1971 shot inside the Clapham Transport Museum, now but a memory; and by a view of **RF146** (**MLL 533**) of 1952, as refurbished at Aldenham Works in May 1967. The picture is at Eccleston Bridge, London, in September 1972. Service 708 to Hemel Hempstead was one of the writer's regular routes from Victoria to Hendon in the 1960s, along with the 706 and 707 to Aylesbury, which together gave a 15-minute headway for the journey. *(Both: G H F Atkins/© John Banks Collection)*

Double-deck coaches have ever been in the minority, even the mighty Green Line never really making a success of the type, though they did reasonably well with more comfortable versions of the Routemaster. Certainly until recent times double-deckers made no impact at all on the private hire and excursion market and such as there were ran on timetabled express routes. More than one Tilling operator found sufficient traffic using certain of its services that coach versions of the Bristol Lodekka were ordered. For its Liverpool to Llandudno express Crosville had had some rear-entrance LD6B versions and by 1962 was taking delivery of 55-seat FLF6Bs, including No. **DFB111** (**144 YFM**), shown at Llandudno *(left)* in July 1970. A year or so later, in October 1971, a later generation of Bristol chassis with Eastern Coach Works bodywork is represented by Standerwick No. **56** (**LRN 56J**) leaving Digbeth Coach Station, Birmingham, for Burnley *(above)*. New earlier that year, the vehicle was of type VRL/LH6L and had 60 seats as well as the usual refreshment and bathroom facilities. It has been suggested that the type's demise was allegedly because when they broke down two relieving single-deckers were required. *(Both: G H F Atkins/© John Banks Collection)*

The double-deck coach revolution really began with Ribble and the Leyland Atlantean Gay Hostesses. Supposedly restricted to 64mph, they were able to make up lost time in the schedule in a manner akin to Bill Hoole at the controls of "Mallard", borne out when the writer, circa 1970, personally clocked one at 85mph on the M1. Number **1264** (**NRN 613**) *(left)*, was a typical example. The Leyland PDR1/1 chassis was bodied as a toilet- and servery-equipped 50-seater by Weymann and entered service in 1960. The Gay Hostesses were primarily intended for use on services to London, although No. 1264 had strayed on to the X21 from Liverpool to Carlisle. A less lavishly equipped version is exemplified by No. **1272** (**RRN 421**) *(right)*, seen at Manchester in September 1969, of a type used on express services within the Ribble operating area, in this case the X43 to Skipton. *(Geoff Coxon; John Banks Collection; G H F Atkins/© John Banks Collection)*

Interesting, but are they coaches? The use of time-served urban double-deckers for tourism was brought to a fine art by the British operator Top Deck Travel, using Bristol Lodekkas, which could be spotted in some exotic and far-flung places. The writer saw one near Venice and has heard of them penetrating the Indian sub-continent. They were regularly seen in such tourist traps as Paris and Volendam, and their drivers were blithely cheerful about their vehicles "going for ever" and "never breaking down". Customers lived, ate and slept in the vehicle, thus obviating hotel expenses. Nobody with any knowledge of the Bristol Lodekka will need to be reminded of its legendary reliability, but it was an act of faith to take them so far afield. Although foreign garages might have been familiar with Gardner engines, it is doubtful if they knew much about the Bristol-manufactured components. But, then, if they never broke down... **892 VFM** *(left)* was an ex-Crosville FS6G model dating from 1962 that was 21 years old when Top Deck Travel started using it. Herren Hoffmann und Schauerte, of Lennestadt, operated the German equivalent *(right)* and no doubt the indigenous pensioned-off urban double-deckers were every bit as reliable as the British Lodekkas. This one, **OE-E 444**, was photographed in Köln in 1988. *(Geoff Coxon; John Banks)*

Coaches for special uses included fleets in service with the armed services, police forces and airlines. The writer recalls with little pleasure being conveyed daily in 1961 between Peel House, off Vauxhall Bridge Road, to Hendon training college in petrol-engined Bedford OBs with austere interiors and a variation on the theme was the prison van with tiny one-person cells and a central entrance in the rear. The Greater Manchester police in 1975 bought a fleet of Duple-bodied Bedford SB5s, **HVM 614-8M**, shown *(above)* on delivery. The airport servicing requirements needed by airlines included buses and coaches in some profusion and a visit to any major airport produced many unusual sightings of purpose-built vehicles, some of which did not conform to the Construction & Use Regulations and did not venture beyond the airport's private roads. Conventional vehicles that did so included a fleet of attractive 24-seat Duple-bodied Bedford VAS5 models, **WUL 251-4N**, acquired by British Airways in September 1974. *(All: John Banks Collection)*

The Bedford VAL was neither the first nor the last three-axle chassis offered to British operators. It was not even the first to have two steering axles, having been preceded by the Leyland Panda and Gnu. Those models, however, had been built in small numbers (only one, indeed, in the case of the Panda), whereas the VAL was to become very popular. Introduced in 1962, the VAL was by around £1,000 the cheapest chassis for 36ft-long coachwork sold in the UK. By 1965, Bedford literature was rather coyly announcing a substantial increase in brake-lining area from 47.6 to 63 square inches. A necessary step, this, for the VAL went well but was rather less good at stopping. It was still selling well in 1970 when Foxall of Bridgenorth put **SNT 925H**, seen above with a subsequent owner, into service with a Plaxton 53-seat body. Although Duple and Plaxton supplied coachwork for most VALs, Thomas Harrington, of Hove, made a spirited effort with the Legionnaire, a design that looked forward to the slab-sided profile later to be so effectively marketed by Van Hool. **LHX 510C** was a 1965 52-seater bought by Brunt, of Hatfield. By 1979, when this picture was taken, it was looking its age and perhaps had not long to go. *(Both: Geoff Coxon)*

LHX 510C

PRIVATE

Foreign chassis with foreign bodywork was by no means a late-twentieth-century phenomenon. They had been around since the dawn of the motor industry and such names as Reo, Chevrolet, Lancia and Opel made an impression in Great Britain. The British manufacturers managed to fend them off in the postwar period, however, for a couple of decades or so until in the seventies Mercedes-Benz, DAF and Volvo began to make serious inroads. A Mercedes-Benz O302 demonstrator, OLH 302E, had been seen on various duties (including the United Counties express service from Nottingham to London) in the late 1960s, and in 1971 the vehicle illustrated above, **DLC 950J**, which had been another O302 demonstrator, joined the Wallace Arnold fleet, where it stayed until 1979. Rarer even than the Mercedes-Benz was **GDU 65L** *(right)*, a Portuguese UTIC U2043, built using AEC Swift running units. UTIC built many complete vehicles based on imported AEC equipment but only nine were exported back to the UK. This one was one of two delivered in August 1972 to Bonas, of Coventry, and had passed to Hogg of Sheffield by the time of this October 1979 photograph. *(Both: Geoff Coxon)*

HOGG

GDU 65L

Coachwork from foreign manufacturers had also not been unheard of on British-made chassis in earlier times, and similarly began a successful infiltration in the 1970s. Notable among these imports were the products of Salvador Caetano from Portugal and Van Hool from Belgium. Caetano coachwork was striking in appearance and in the UK was marketed, and badged, as the Moseley Continental by Moseley Group (PSV) Ltd, of Loughborough. These two Caetano 53-seaters *(above)*, **NWU 128/9M**, were on Bedford YRT chassis and were August 1973 deliveries into the fleet of Hargreaves, of Morley, as fleet numbers **128/9**. Van Hool's products were as characteristically "continental" as were Caetano's until Van Hool smoothed its proportions down with such handsome designs as the Alizée. This 49-seat offering *(right)* on a Ford R226 chassis, with its stepped front roofline and "observation" windows was rather odd, though that feature aside its lines were more distinguished than that of the contemporary Caetano. **JVD 981L** was new in January 1973 to J Beaton, of High Blantyre, Lanarkshire. *(Both: Geoff Coxon)*

Heavyweights new and second-hand were really the backbone of British coaching, no matter how hard the salesmen from Luton and Dagenham tried. The major company operators and many of the larger independents would have nothing else, and even when lightweights did appear in such fleets, they were usually in penny numbers and bought for a specific purpose, such as local tour and excursion work. Such purchases were more often than not written down over a short period and sold on, sometimes after only one or two seasons' work. The Leyland Leopard was one of the giants of the underfloor-engined heavyweight list and among the more attractive examples were those with Alexander coachwork. The Scottish Bus Group companies had many, Western SMT's in a simple black and white colour scheme with scroll fleetnames being among the most attractive. The example shown above, No. **2499** (**GCS 792N**), dated from 1975. The Tilling companies, though not obliged to buy Eastern Coach Works-bodied Bristol chassis, nearly always did, and the rear-engined Bristol RE was a popular choice for express services. Because of their solid engineering, heavyweight coaches often had a lot of life in them when withdrawn, and the canny independent could pick up a bargain, as did Gardiner Brothers *(right)*, of Spennymoor, with former Eastern National **GVW 982H**. *(Both: Geoff Coxon)*

Vanished names among the heavyweights include AEC and Duple. Who would have believed that in the summer of 1977 when R & M Bissett, of Ryton, added **XUP 157R** *(above)* to their "Primrose" fleet? Of all the photographs in this book, it may be that none exemplifies better all that was traditional in the British coaching industry at that time than this sunlit view of an AEC Reliance. Perhaps lacking the ultimate in maximum speed (and accompanying sound effects) of the turbocharged Fords, the Reliance was solid and dignified and might well last a lot longer. When treated to a conservative but well-designed livery, there were few vehicles around that brought more credit to their owners. At around this time Bissett had a fleet of ten, nine of which were AECs and all but this one with Plaxton coachwork. *(Geoff Coxon)*

Heavyweight lookalikes really did look the same from the outside, as proved by Southern of Barrhead's 53-seat Ford R1114 **RDS 250W**, a 1980 delivery, again bodied by Duple *(right)*. Inside, however, for both driver and passenger, a heightened mechanical noise would have been evident. Fords with turbochargers were undeniably fast but they could wear out quickly under intensive use. *(John Banks Collection)*

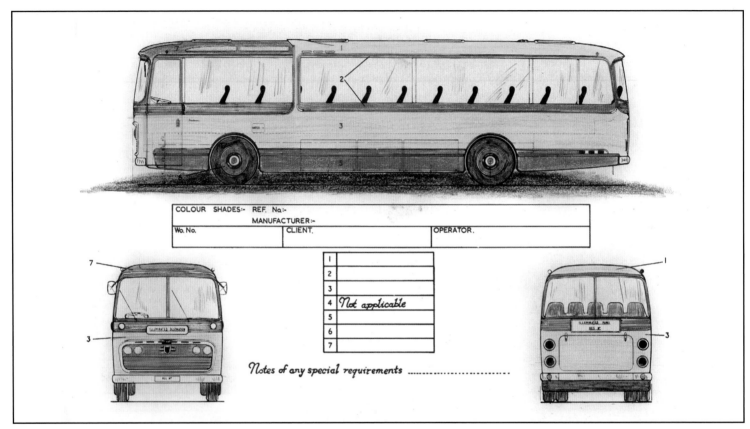

COLOUR SHADES:- REF. No.:-
MANUFACTURER:-

Wo. No.	CLIENT.	OPERATOR.

1	
2	
3	
4	*Not applicable*
5	
6	
7	

Notes of any special requirements ....

Ordering new coaches could involve some difficult decisions: lightweight or heavyweight? British or foreign chassis? Van Hool, Duple, Plaxton coachwork? keep the livery or change it?... For the late Hubert Allen, however, it was easy, for after the mid sixties he bought little other than Plaxton-bodied AEC Reliances. Everything about Yelloway, at least until Hubert Allen's involvement ceased, was traditional, especially the livery. That he did have thoughts of alternative colour schemes, however, is made clear by these fascinating documents, coloured in in Hubert's own hand. Blank line-drawings were supplied by Plaxton to customers, who used them to indicate their livery requirements, and in this case they referred to a batch of Plaxton Panorama Reliances being ordered for delivery to Yelloway in 1968, which entered service as KDK 800-5F. On this page, Hubert experimented with a scheme that was eventually rejected for that shown on the opposite page. *(Both: John Banks Collection)*

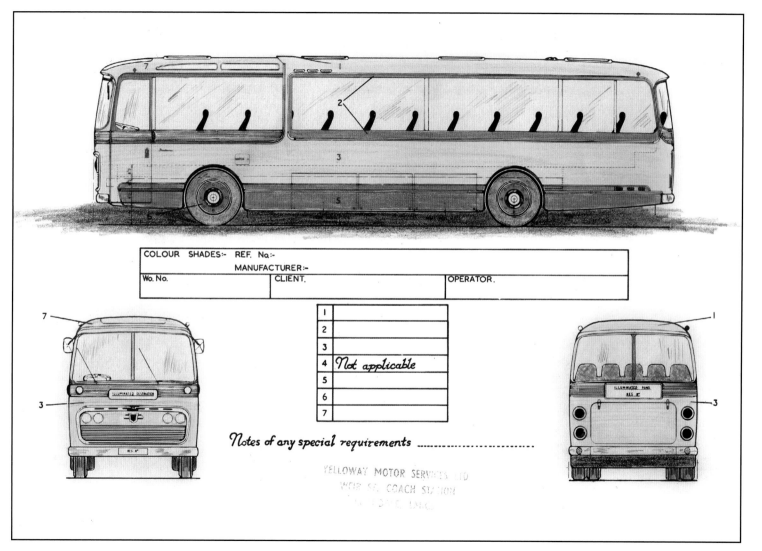

COLOUR SHADES:- REF. No:-
MANUFACTURER:-

Wo. No.	CLIENT.	OPERATOR.

1	
2	
3	
4	*Not applicable*
5	
6	
7	

Notes of any special requirements ....

YELLOWAY MOTOR SERVICES LTD
WEIR St. COACH STATION

The handing-over ceremony, accompanied on occasion by lunch and a tour of the works, saw the order for a new coach translated into reality, and for a while there was that wonderful *ambience* (compounded as much of smell and feel as of appearance and performance) of "brand-new" that would soon disappear and could never reappear, no matter how meticulously a vehicle was maintained and repaired. Illustrated on the left is **KVL 78P**, a 1975 Duple-bodied Bedford YRT 53-seater, being handed over for use in the fleet of R J Eaglen & Son, trading as Eagre Coaches, of Morton, Lincolnshire.

Official photography, either by the chassis maker or coachbuilder, or sometimes by the new owner, often preceded or followed the handing over. On the odd occasion a suitable "temporary" number plate was affixed. At right is "**PRE 1M**" of Mercer's (Longridge) Ltd, which was connected with Premier Motor Tours (Preston) Ltd. The 1974 Duple-bodied Bedford YRT was probably UTC 113M. Behind it is a similarly liveried 45-seat Bedford YRQ bearing the "Premier" fleetname and a "UTC" registration, doubtless UTC 115M. The two operators had UTC 111-5M in early 1974 - all Bedfords but of three different models (a VAS5, three YRTs and a YRQ). *(Both: John Banks Collection)*

Brand new coaches make good photographs, often helped in more recent times by the more imaginative of the modern liveries. A single base colour with a cream waistrail (and, perhaps, a cream or white roof), and even more restrained liveries, gave way in many fleets to angled stripes and mixed-and-matched shades in combinations calculated to send an interior decorator into terminal decline. When these effusions were augmented by pictures of sunsets, seascapes and bikini-clad females one might have been forgiven for thinking that the phenomenon had gone quite far enough. Some of the "angled-stripes" liveries worked well, however, including from 1988 *(above)* those on Harry Shaw of Coventry's Duple-bodied Volvo (**E31 MKV**) and Mayne of Buckie's Dennis Javelin (one of E980/90 KJF). *(John Banks Collection)*

Attendance at coach rallies was a logical step after the selection, ordering, handing over and commissioning of a new coach (some even went directly from the coachbuilder). Brighton and Blackpool were equally logical as locations for such events, which lifted - for a weekend - the entire concept of coaching several orders of magnitude above the day-to-day grind of schools, works contracts and day trips that most of the coaches would very soon be thrown into. Indeed, it was one of the sorrows of the industry (and of our hobby) to see rally winners a dozen or so years later in various states of decrepitude or - worse - in the scrapyard. The future was bright, however, for entry number 33 at the 28th British Coach Rally in Brighton in 1982. **TPE 170X** *(right)* was a Setra S215H with Kässbohrer 53-seat coachwork, originally a Setra demonstrator but quickly sold to Stone, of Church Gresley, Derbyshire. *(Geoff Coxon)*

Municipal operation of coaches was perhaps the rarest such use. It had not been unknown in regulated days for coaches to be ordered for specific uses, for example as the town's "committee coach", but following deregulation some municipalities joined in the free-for-all and went looking for work that had hitherto been outside their normal sphere. This did not go down too well among traditional coach operators but the changes were the will of politicians who, one often thinks, could not have known very much about the road passenger-carrying industry, and there was no longer protection from or recourse to the Traffic Commissioners. An entirely legitimate, albeit short-lived, use of Leyland Leopard coaches by Nottingham City Transport *(above)* was in connection with park and ride services, for which 18 Duple Dominant-bodied 49-seaters were purchased in April 1975. Known as "Lilac Leopards" because of the livery, 14 of them were sold to Maidstone Borough Transport the following year. Number **17** (**HNU 117N**) was photographed in July 1975. Lancaster City Transport *(right)* was also a user of the Leyland Leopard, No. **18** (**MFR 18P**) of 1976 having an Alexander 49-seat body. *(G H F Atkins/© John Banks Collection; Geoff Coxon)*

Coach stations and coach parks were magnets for the enthusiast photographer, who quickly worked out where the parking areas were and which categories of operator used them. In some cases, all operators were mingled together, but there were cases of "us and them" arrangements. In Scarborough the independents parked at William Street while their private hire parties had their day or half-day in the resort. In this view *(above)* the first vehicle is a great rarity. Skills of Nottingham No. **67** (**RTV 667G**) was a Leyland Panther with Plaxton 51-seat coachwork. This was September 1973 and most of the other 30 or so coaches - chassis and bodywork - were of British manufacture. Victoria Coach Station *(right)* was where London express services arrivals and departures were concentrated. In this September 1972 view, Yorkshire Traction and East Yorkshire were fielding Leyland Leopards, United Counties a Bristol RE and East Kent an AEC Reliance. Nearly four years into the National era, there was as yet little outward evidence. Things were to change very quickly and dramatically. *(Both: G H F Atkins/© John Banks Collection)*

Coaches in town and country and everywhere in between were part of the fascination. A vehicle that had been in Paris on Sunday might well be carrying schoolchildren to the swimming baths in Stevenage the following Monday. There has been discussion as long as this writer can remember as to exactly what constitutes a "dual-purpose" vehicle: perhaps the truest definition lies in what the owner of the vehicle wanted to do with it. One often shuddered at seeing the aforementioned schoolchildren making a dustbin of the interior of a new Volvo or Leyland Leopard that was due to go on a prestigious private hire after the swimming job, but the owner had to keep the wheels turning to meet the hire purchase payments and the driver had a mop and bucket in the side lockers. Luxury coaches on stage services were a relatively common feature, too, exemplified by 1977 OK Motor Services Leyland Leopard Duple 53-seater **WGR 510R** on its way out of Newcastle to Bishop Auckland. The Tyneside scene contrasts with rural Essex and **YHA 334X** from the Wiffen, of Finchingfield, fleet. A 1982 Ford R1014, this immaculate little vehicle had Plaxton 33-seat coachwork. *(Both: Geoff Coxon)*

It is easy, some years on, to forget just how all-enveloping was the *National Bus Company* for so long following its foundation on 1st January 1969. All the former British Electrical Traction Group and Tilling Group coach fleets were painted in a scarcely imaginative all-over white livery with the word NATIONAL in alternate red and blue plain block letters. A double "N" symbol, shaped to look like an arrow, was added, sometimes the wrong way round. The loss of so much local identity and goodwill, usually built up over many decades of service, was considered in some quarters to be unwise and the subsidiary company fleetnames were added, albeit in smaller lettering, as on East Kent's 1974 AEC Reliance **GFN 558N**, *(this page)*, which had Duple 55-seat coachwork. A decade or so later *(right)* ideas of what was needed for express services had moved on, and from the Yorkshire Traction fleet we have fleet number **92**, a six-wheeled Auwaerter Neoplan new in 1986 as C92 KET and reregistered **HE 5362**. It was at Chesterfield in June 1991 on its way to London. *(John Banks Collection; G H F Atkins/© John Banks Collection)*

Spanish coaching on the Costa Brava usually meant, apart from the hordes of British and other foreign shuttle coaches, Pegaso chassis with exotic coachwork used on what we would think of as limited stop inter-urban services. The scenic view dates from 1985, taken in the sort of day-in-day-out summer weather that makes the region so attractive to British tourists. On the opposite page is a *Sarfa Costa Brava* Pegaso seen in Gerona on 20th July 1992, having just arrived from La Escala on the coast. *(Both: John Banks)*

Coaches from Eastern Europe ... Following the relaxation of state control and the eventual collapse of communism in Eastern Europe, coaches from those countries increasingly appeared in the popular tourist destinations. These two, seen in Paris on 31st August 1990, were from Hungary and Czechoslovakia; conversations with their drivers provided first-hand evidence of just how different a world it had been and, to some extent, still was, particularly with regard to wages and conditions, behind the Iron Curtain. *(Both: John Banks)*

Articulated coaches were not as common on the Continent as the equivalent service bus version (in an era that predated the fatuous expression "bendibus"), but there were some. Not at that time being a type that the United Kingdom, as ever somewhat tardy in taking advantage of such advances, generally allowed, sightings of them abroad were appreciated, and if the camera was to hand ... It was on 5th November 1986, when Henri de Boeck's Van Hool-bodied MAN was spotted in Brussels. With its understated beige livery, it was a very impressive vehicle. A chat with its driver brought forth the information that the vehicle handled very well and that it gave no difficulty in city traffic. *(Both: John Banks)*

67

Driver training was handled in a variety of ways, from the fully fleged courses at such hallowed etablishments as London Transport's Chiswick, that included several days of classroom theory before the steering wheel was even touched, to the smaller independent's "you'd better swat up on the Highway Code the night before your driving test". Specialist driving schools for public service vehicle drivers have played their part and some interesting vehicles have been used. The Lamm *écol'auto* (driving school) in Mulhouse, Alsace, was using this Unic coach *(left)* for such work on 31st October 1993. *(John Banks)*

The driving cab of a new coach became ever more complicated as the decades rolled on and officialdom threw ever more restrictive legislation at motor vehicles and their users. The instrumentation and aids to comfort vouchsafed the driver of the older Bedfords, AEC Regals and Leyland Tigers shown on earlier pages were rather sparse compared with the technological wonder that was the Duple Integral 425. There are well over two dozen items demanding the driver's attention, but then he also had power steering, powerful, easily operated braking and a simple air-operated handbrake, as well as a comfortable seat with comprehensive adjustment and arm- and headrests. This example had a manual gearbox but other coaches in more recent times have also had automatic transmissions of one sort or another, making life even easier. *(John Banks Collection)*

Comfort for the passengers was not so easy to improve on, not being legislation-driven as were many of the changes to the driver's environment. Coaches with sleeping berths, toilets and refreshment facilities were on the road long before the 1939-45 war. Standards of interior trim and seating comfort were very high and, if anything, declined with the move from hand-crafted items made by artisans from traditional materials such as fine hardwoods and leather towards machine mass production using plastics and man-made fibres. Conversely, in the earlier period, driver comfort was often little considered. Inside the saloon, however, it had all been seen before: curtains, tables, buffet bars, toilets, radio "entertainment"; but more recently those facilities were differently marketed, and "Executive" coaches became popular. These moved with the times, and it was not long before videotape, and then DVD, players and television sets were a part of the specification. In the views above, of **HER 667N**, a 1975 Bedford YRT with Duple 40-seat coachwork, the provision of reversed seating, tables and servery are illustrated. Such seating made it awkward for guides, whose "on the left we now see..." was confusing for half of the passengers. Serveries equipped with spirits optics, too, could give rise to some awkwardness at customs checkpoints. The plain, less-gadget-equipped but very welcoming and luxurious Duple 57-seat interior on the right is of Volvo B10M **E31 MKV** of Harry Shaw, Coventry. *(All: John Banks Collection)*

Winter was the time for acquiring second-hand vehicles and readying them for the coming season. In this case, a couple of ex-Park's of Hamilton Volvo B10Ms with Van Hool coachwork were undergoing the metamorphosis from the original, rather trendy, maroon and cream stripes to Halcyon Travel's bright yellow. *(All: John Banks)*

although use of the toilet was allowed *gratis*. Such incidents were invariably serious, for the driver's hours maxima were as a matter of course scheduled as the norm, and there was not much by way of allowance for unforeseen delays. The lower view illustrates that scourge of Paris in the 1980s, *la manif (une manifestation* = protest march). On this occasion in 1986 near *les Tuileries*, one had brought the centre of Paris to a standstill. During these dramas there was nothing to do in either case save sit back, wait patiently and hope that the problems would clear before the schedule was irretrievably damaged. In Paris, this was done pleasantly at a nearby pavement café while the protest passed on towards the Elysée Palace. *(Both: John Banks)*

The operation by British operators of coach services abroad, whether on overnight shuttles to the warm south or tours to the great cities, can bring incidents and circumstances that throw the schedules awry. Even such familiar matters as traffic jams on motorways or protestors demonstrating in a capital city can have more serious ramifications if encountered abroad; no doubt it is the same for foreign operators bringing their vehicles to the UK. In the picture above, a major accident involving a number of lorries had caused traffic to grind to a halt on an Italian motorway near Milan. The delay was such that the tailback stretched for 60 miles. Under the merciless noonday sun becalmed drivers and passengers were out of their cars and a brisk business was done supplying them with coffee and chilled drinks from the coach servery,

British coaches of foreign manufacture, especially the popular Van Hool-bodied Volvos, in use on the European mainland seldom seemed out of place, but it was a different matter when a British chassis/body combination (or in this case a British-built integral vehicle) was put into service in left-hand drive form by a foreign operator. This Duple 425, registered AG 7028 in the Aargau canton of Switzerland, is believed to be Duple chassis number LSDA 1512/109. *(John Banks Collection)*

Yesterday's future...

...that somehow did not come to pass. Six-wheeled double-deckers became, with very few exceptions, the ultimate. Coach Lines of Warrington's Neoplan Skyliner **465 FBC**, typical of the genre, had conveyed a party of schoolchildren and staff from Wolverhampton to Sorrento. It is seen alongside the Bay of Naples *(left)* on 28th June 1992. The logical extension of the Neoplan was to an eight-wheeled Super-Skyliner and, indeed, plans were drawn up for a 14.36 metre 54-seater *(right)*. Three of these are reported as having run in Chile and two in Argentina. The latter, at least, were shipped to South America as rolling shells built up to upper-deck floor level and completed by the coachbuilder Cametal. The Super-Skyliner was later developed into the Megaliner. A mythical beast, then, the rigid eight-wheeler, and one had small hope of seeing one in Europe until, quite out of the blue, the white, grey and pink vision seen on the following page confronted the photographer outside Mulhouse, Alsace, railway station on 27th January 1994. Another development was the articulated eight-wheeled Neoplan N138/4 Jumbocruiser *(see Page 79)*, in this case running for a Stavanger, Norway, operator and seen at Keukenhof Gardens, Holland, on 23rd April 1986. The forward section contained the power unit, although one of the few built was powered from the rear section. The Jumbocruiser had a potential seating capacity of 144, but this example held a mere 90. The coach park at Keukenhof at tulip time was an international melting pot and many interesting types and models were encountered. This sighting, however, remains unique for the writer as, so far, does that of the rigid eight-wheeled Megaliner. *(All: John Banks)*

John Banks Collection/Gottlob Auwärter GMBH

Today's Way Forward? Bringing the story right up to date is Hodson's **EC02 BUS**, a silent, clean, battery-powered Renault seen operating in Lincoln on tourist duties on Friday, 13th May 2005. *(John Banks)*